these
unforgettable
things

Also by s.l. gray

Skin, Bones, and Too Much Love

these
unforgettable
things

-s.l. gray

these unforgettable things
Copyright © 2021 Samantha Gray

IBSN: 9798703278581

Independently published by Samantha Gray

Cover art by Merethe Liljedahl
Cover design by Samantha Gray

for my mother

for one

I clawed at those hands,
dug my heels into the dirt,
resisted the pull
as much as I could

like I always do,

but still
I crossed
another finish line.

This is me writing pages and pages
of all the things I wanted to tell you,

when I agreed that all was said and done.

I still remember
what
your voice sounds like

when you are in love
and when you
no longer are.

You are leaving this place
without leaving anything behind,

your next home will be full.

Sorrow will not fill an empty space and ask:
"Where did the warmth that was here before go?"

"Why did it go?"

You cannot say
that this is just as hard for you
as it is for me.

At best,
we were in love.

At worst,
it did not tell us
we could make ourselves
at home in it.

I thought our fire blazed
too bright and heavy
for anything to extinguish us.

Look at us now:

smoke
curling up to the sky
blown away
with the wind
to nothing.

When I said
I did not mind
remembering you
as you once were,
it was during those
blissful moments
when I thought
I would know
who you are
always.

I rearrange everything here.

There is always an empty space
like it is another solid thing
I carried to a different spot.

Something is missing.

I try to convince myself
it is not you.

You told me
don't take it to heart,

as if it was not
one of the many things
you called yours,

and the only thing
you did not take with you.

They say lightning
never strikes
the same place twice
and I think that is why
I find it so hard
to let you go.

In another life,
you know you have not met all of me.

You know that I will forever be growing
and you do not want to miss any of it.

We hold each other a bit tighter,
and letting go of this love
is not something you want to do.

It is not something I have to do.

It runs around here
wildly,

*the thought of your hands
reaching for
someone else.*

I keep dreaming of a closed door.

It always takes too long to open,
and I awake before you
or anything else I have lost
can return to me.

I called your name
to pull you back to me,
and it looked like
I had pulled you out
of a dream.

Maybe that is why
I am still so haunted
by you.

How often I have awoken from dreams of you
to find regret standing in the doorway
wanting to climb into bed with me
like a child broken free from a nightmare,

but it is not small, and it is not afraid.

And I wish that I could say I love(d) you
just enough to get up and
turn it away every single time,
but some nights my heart was
too heavy to stand.

I could do nothing but watch
as it made its way over
and wrapped its arms around me.

I forget
what the dream
was about,

I just remember
seeing your face.

I am jealous of the ones
that came into your life
when I did,

not like the way I did,

and are still with you
when I am not.

I used to be the one
that knew you the most.

Now when they ask me
how you are,

I have to tell them
I am wondering too.

Your hands
became unsteady
and I watched
as everything you loved
about me
fell away from you.

You were once so sure of me.

I never wanted to take anything
from your hands,

just to place my own in them.

I will not reduce what we were.

They tell me I should,
tell me that it is easy,
that it will make this easier.

And I ask them to show me
how someone reaches up to steal
the sun from out of the sky
and reduce it to a candle flame
to be snuffed out.

They do not know what this love was,
they do not get to tell me how long
I should mourn.

I would never
choose to forget you
even if someone else
swore to me that they
could give me a mind
with better memories.

I let you go,

but I have been
emptying my pockets
into fountains and wells,
and turning my face
towards the night sky,

wishing and wishing
for you to come back.

*Does that still make me
selfless?*

I did not count down the days,
(sometimes I wonder if you had been).

No, the day would end,
and I would recall it,
and wonder how many more
I would get with you.

We both could not see forever,
but only one of us could see the end.

I told loss that I did not want to know it.

It told me: *to become ignorant of loss*
you must forget the one you lost.

And I wondered at that moment
if I would ever again be mesmerized
by someone's ability to draw me out
of the person I thought I should be
but did not want to become.

And I remembered laughing with you
about how many times I said
I would choose you
that we lost count.

I can still hear our laugher
as I do this one last time.

One day
I will find myself
in a place
where I will think of you
in the past
and not wish to go back.

The light will return,
and I will not use it
to look for you again.

I will probably always carry you with me,
but I will gather so much more
as I continue this journey.

*Right now, it feels like you are my life,
eventually, you will only be a part of it.*

It has been three days since your birthday,
and I do not reach for the phone.

It is not the idea of wishing happiness
to the one who said
they could no longer give me any
that keeps my hands folded.

(I am never not wishing you happiness.)

It is the thought of placing myself
into another year of your life
when you walked away from me in the one before.

(You are still walking away, and I should be too.)

I wrote down all those plans we made
and tucked them away between the pages
of all my other favorite fictional stories.

they were once so real.

I made a mistake believing
I would only feel love
when you held me.

You do not reach for me again,
but love,
love does.

I do not call it a mistake to have loved you, but I did not know what else to call the way I lived off that love when they asked me what I would do now that you are gone, and I could not find any words. *I could not even imagine it.*

I hope your heart
makes up its mind
someday,

even if it does not
decide on me.

I can still find you in places,
but I no longer wish to stay
longer than I intended.

I can still find you in things,
but I no longer want to pick them up
and take them with me.

It took me a while to be able
to put you down
and not return for you.

To not want you so strongly
that you felt necessary to me.

You were at the forefront,
but you were not my only dream.

~~In another life~~
In this life
I will find something
to dream of other than
all the ways
we could have been.

and now we carry so little
of all we knew of one another.

The empty spaces
are filled again,
but sometimes I think
I catch you still there
from the corner of my eye.

I am a glass that healing
as poured itself halfway into.

Which is to say

I still reach for you
in the morning,
but when my hand falls
through that empty space,

I do not wish for you
to travel back here
I just hope that you
have made it somewhere safe.

I always leaned into you when I was laughing,
like a plant growing towards the sun.

My life was beautiful with you in it,
and I have found beauty in it after you.

(know that there was a dark space
between those two
that I had to get through.)

I will always remember you,

but when I am reminded of
all that time we spent together

I no longer wish that we had more of it.

I am only thankful
that I can face something unforgettable
with a smile.

I no longer wonder
where you went.

Your footsteps
are getting farther
and farther away
from where you left me,

and now
so are my own.

I found a photo of us,

You lay not too far from me,
your hand was stretching out
reaching for me,

and my heart did not skip a beat
at the sight of us,
at the sight of all that love it had once known.

Your hand has not been in reach
for some time,
but I have finally let it go.

though no longer for you and I,
there is still so much more time.

for another

I did not want this to be a lesson
I wanted this to be love.

I do not wish that we had never met,
but it is good that we are

strangers again.

The words used to be much softer for you
back when I was in love and lost in you.

Now you want an apology
for what I have done to them.

My heart is still a forgiving thing,
but there has been no apology
for what you have done to it,

and there will be no apology
for the way I am healing it.

For the way I am finding my way out of you.

It still sends a chill
down my spine,

knowing the way
someone you love
can change into someone
you do not know
anymore.

You floated away
from me so slowly,

made me believe
you had given me time
to try and reel you
back in,

but you always knew
you were not going to bite.

If I had known
when I met you that you
would absorb my sun,

I would have pulled
my hands away
from your reaching ones.

You would have never
taken all the light
and warmth with you.

I dug a grave after
I said I could not
live without you

threw those words in
and walked away.

I have not forgotten
what it was like
to be loved by you.

So when you say
I miss you

I know what
you really mean is
I miss parts of you.

You say
I am heartless.

I hear:
*You gave me your heart
and I did not care for it.*

There is a bottle of perfume
I can no longer use,
it is filled with nothing but memories
that smell just like you.

You found one last way to reach me
and you chose to dig your nails in.

You closed the door
behind you
and it did not
echo through me.

I have been filled
with so much more
than the love
you took for granted.

There are
unaddressed letters
scattered all over house.

I write
and write
and write
to the person
you were before.

I have no desire
to bring this love
back to life,

but still, I carry grief.

There was love in me
for you

but also hurt in me
from you.

I am now a body
filled with neither.

A heavy
and light thing
all at once.

I remember staring down at my empty hands,

and like opening a book to the same page
over and over
my palms always read:

"When are you going to stop waiting to be saved
by the one who is slowly killing you?"

And it was the fear that those words
could brand my skin if I let them,

it was knowing that you held
all I had given you
along with everything you could have given me
but never would

that had my hands curling into fists,

ready to fight for fullness again.
ready to save myself.

to be clear:
being yours
was (barely)
a second identity.

I am always mine first.

I might always be
restless with want,

but you have
made me weary
of what
I am being handed.

How odd it is
to still feel
the hold of someone
who never
made me feel
wanted.

The ground has split between us.

I spent a long-time questioning
why you chose to do the things you did,
and where, if you had any,
had you hidden your remorse.

There was no echo of any answers
drifting over the abyss,
and I had to let go of the need to know
before I fell into it.

and it is knowing I will forgive you one day,
and the only one who will need that
is me.

I told you
I never let myself
think of you,

and it was so strange
to see running water
look like
an abandoned thing.

I let the pain in and it tore me apart.
It left with all those heavy pieces of you.

You said I would be empty after you,

but that only meant I would be without
all the pain you caused me.

That only meant that I was making space
for healing
and the love I deserve.

There were only so many times
you could cut me open
and try to use love as a bandage
to stop the bleeding.

Eventually, it seeped through it.

Eventually, I saw through you.

The journey to love myself
was a long, trying, but vital one.

Telling me I had a hand
in the pain you caused me
was never going to be
accepted.

Your door is closed.

I am not fighting
to be let back in,

and you do not stay
close enough
on the other side
to hear if I even tried.

They will make a note of you,

of how you pushed the sun down
and yanked the path toward the future I planned
from beneath my feet
and directed me toward an uncertain one.

how despite the loss,
                    the darkness,
                            and the uncertainty
I was merely slowed down
I was not stopped.

They will scribble down my name
and write
            always moving forward
beneath it.

I would never pause my life
whenever you stepped out of it.

Coming back to me
will never the same
as going back
in time.

I am glad
that you have found
so much to love
after all the destruction.

It means that I was not
the end for you,
and you were not
the end for me.

It blew across
an ocean that was calm
(that was healed).

It was nothing more
than a disturbance.

Your voice
breaking the silence.

I gave myself to you wholly,
and in the end
I had to get myself back
piece
   by
     piece.

If I could say anything to you now,
it would be:

it does not make someone incomplete
just because they cannot give you
what you are lacking.

Though I do not know
in what form,

I know the warmth
will arrive again.

The space you once claimed
next to me
will not always be cold.

And just like you,

I thought the hurt
would never leave.

And just like you,

it touched me one last time
and turned into a memory.

I can forgive you for the wreckage,

but I cannot forget
the way I was torn down.

I am a rebuilt home,
and you are not allowed back in.

I created a bouquet
of the forgiveness
that bloomed within me
and laid it down upon
the empty grave
of your promises.

They say unforgettable things are *remarkable, special, and spectacular,* yet I call you unforgettable because it is important for me to remember being hurt. *It is important to remember the way I will never allow myself to be treated again.*

I am still giving gratitude to all those lovely beings I knew before you. Still praising the praising I saw when they appraised the flaws I let breathe in front of them. Still celebrating their gentle hold that I can still feel even after being in your suffocating one. Still admiring the memorialization of the way they loved me that will never let me fall for a deception.

I am walking away
not as the person I was before
and not as the person
I hoped I would become with you,

but still as someone worthy of love.

I hope one day you can tell someone
you love them without using it as an excuse.

I hope one day you can tell someone
you love them when they are not expecting
an apology first.

I hope one day you can tell someone
you love them and they will not look back
and wonder if you are being honest.

I hope one day you will understand
what love truly is.

for myself

You and that heart
always make it through.

Love asked me,
"How will you hold me?"

I replied, *"Gently."*

It asked, *"And if I have to go?"*

I crossed my fingers
behind my back
and said, *"I will let you."*

Losing love has never
felt like a hand
simply slipping
from my own.

*The nails always dig in
and tear away.*

If the pain could speak
I know it would say,

*You know nothing
lasts forever.*

I know it would ask,

*Must you always hold on
to everything so tightly.*

So, the love left,

we do not need
to replace it with hate.

*It only adds more space
to the emptiness.*

They say goodbye,
and it feels like I cross oceans
before I can say it back.

Hope puts me back on my feet
tells me I am not done yet.

I think there is
a lot of happiness
out there in the world,

I think one day
some of it
will be mine to keep.

It is getting harder to hear her now,
   that girl I used to be,
but I know she is still telling me
to keep going.

Wait for them if you must,
but do not let them keep you
in one place.

I apologized to my heart
for wanting nothing
but more of something
that has ended.

I can let them all go,

but I might always
walk into a crowd
and search for the eyes
of everyone that I have lost.

I can let them all go,

but I might always wonder
where they went
and hope it was not too far.

I still miss a love that is long gone
and that is okay.

The day comes to an end, and it tells me
it is all right that I have done nothing with it
but remember.

I want to hold everything I love
and move forward without caution.

Not every white flag is easy to wave. There are things we do not ever want to be done with but need to put an end to.

I do not know exactly
how much strength it takes
to tell something
you still wish could stay with you,
even though it has become
bad for you,
that it is time to go.

It felt like a lot.

There is no time limit to healing;
you take as much of it as you need.

I will never be fond of the feeling of empty hands when they once held so much, but I have an even deeper aversion to hands that hold on to things in need of freedom.

perhaps these dreams of ours
are working towards us, too.

And I have fought to keep a love alive
that I believed was not dying.

And I have pried my hands apart
from someone that wore the face of love
but did not know how to speak its language.

And I have turned my palms up
and let go of a love
that could not stretch it wings with me.

And still, I believe that there is a love
that will tuck its hand in mine
and never let go.

Despite it all,

      my heart is still

           a forgiving thing.

My mother raised me
with love,

fed it to me,

told me
never starve yourself of it.

One day you will find that dream
you thought would never be yours

within arm's reach
waiting for you.

My body holds my heart,
thus, supporting every other vital part of me.
what right did I have to tell it
that it was not the right kind?

remember:

not every change
will feel like an intruder.

In a dream I apologized
to the girl
I used to be.

I told her,

you could have been loved
if only
I had let you be.

You will not find new happiness
by wondering what it looks like
for the one you have lost.

I have found that happiness never withers
without the intention to bloom again.

We will not always
be torn open by
these unforgettable things.

When they leave
the space you gave them,

stretch yourself out further.

take it back.

We eventually learn how
to close wounds
without closure.

It is okay if you need time to forgive.
It is okay if you are unable to.
It is okay if the only thing you want to give
is time for yourself to heal
from what they say you need to give forgiveness to.

You will heal

when you are
ready to

not when they say
you should.

I am committed to myself
to this regrowth.

They say I am
my mother's daughter.

Which is to say,
there is another fire
that cannot be put out.

never let anyone
        get in the way
                of your continuation.

Our hearts cannot grow stronger
without knowing the feeling of pain,
just as wildflowers cannot stand tall
without the showers of rain.

You do not have to settle into a life
you did not dream or expect to live.

You can always
always
change it.

We will build a home
around the love we find,

leave all the windows
and doors wide open,

trust in each other
that it will see the way out,

and choose to settle in.

I stopped romanticizing the idea
that I was missing something
that one someone else could give me.

I can make space for someone else
but I will still be felt everywhere.

I am not the person
I want to be yet.

I am trying not to be
too hard on the one
I am now.

I know you,

you with your arms
always open.

You do not know
where the love
will come from next,

but you are always ready
to embrace it,

to catch it.

I no longer think
the absence of a goodbye
means it is not over.

I still look back,

    but I have stopped

        r e a c h i n g.

I can say with certainty now
that if you could shout into me
there would be no echo.

This day holds a new beginning,
and I will not take it for granted.

I will place my worth, my dreams,
my strength, and hope among
these unforgettable things.

end.

(this is the ending of one healing story.
have you written yours yet?)

Acknowledgements

I have been blessed with too much in my life not to thank God for it all. Thank you to my mother, whose strength and endurance truly astounds me. You are here to read this and that makes this book mean so much more. Thank you to my siblings, who have always treated my writing like it is something spectacular. They do not know how much higher they have lifted me. Thank you to my readers who have wanted this book to exist. For giving my words so many homes.

Thank you. Thank you. Thank you.

Other places to find S.L. Gray:

 @s.l._gray

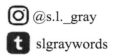 slgraywords